HOW YOUR BODY WORKS

Sensing the World

by Philip Morgan

amicus

Published by Amicus
P.O. Box 1329, Mankato, Minnesota 56002

Printed in the United States of America, at Corporate Graphics
in North Mankato, Minnesota

Library of Congress Cataloging-in-Publication Data
Morgan, Philip.
  Sensing the world / Philip Morgan.
     p. cm. -- (How your body works)
  Summary: "Discusses the different senses of the human body, and how each work together and on their own"--Provided by publisher.
  Includes index.
  ISBN 978-1-60753-056-5 (lib. bdg.)
  1. Senses and sensation--Juvenile literature. 2. Sense organs--Juvenile literature. I. Title.
  QP434.M667 2011
  612.8--dc22

                                                            2009047339

Created by Appleseed Editions, Ltd.
Designed by Helen James
Edited by Mary-Jane Wilkins
Artwork by Graham Rosewarne
Picture research by Su Alexander
Consultant: Steve Parker

Photograph acknowledgements
page 4 Brigitte Sporrer/Corbis; 7 Michael Keller/Corbis; 8 Omikron/Science Photo Library; 9 Montreal Neurological Institute/Science Photo Library; 12 Steve Gschmeissner/Science Photo Library; 13 Sovereign, ISM/Science Photo Library; 14 Patrik Giardino/Corbis; 15 Annabella Bluesky/Science Photo Library; 17 Christine Schneider/Corbis; 26 Bryan and Cherry Alexander/Alamy; 27 Darama/Corbis; 18 Jean-Pierre Lescourret/Corbis; 19 David White/Alamy; 21 Frontline Photography/Alamy; 22 Foodfolio/Alamy; 23 Erick Nguyen/Alamy; 25 LWA-Dann Tardif/Corbis; 28 Simon Marcus/Corbis; 29 A.Inden/Corbis
Front cover Sovereign, ISM/Science Photo Library

DAD0037
32010

9 8 7 6 5 4 3 2 1

Contents

What's Around You?

Imagine that you couldn't see the sky or hear a friend's voice. What would it be like if you couldn't smell your favorite meal, or taste a tropical fruit? How could you live without touching people and things? Your senses give you important information about the world around you.

Five Senses

You have five senses that give you lots of details about what's happening around you. Each sense responds to something in the environment. Your eyes respond to light rays and tell you whether the sky is blue or if there are clouds bringing rain. Your ears respond to sound waves and

We use our sense organs all the time for looking at, hearing, tasting, smelling, and touching the things around us.

tell you about the tone of people's voices —they can tell you whether a voice is a familiar friend's or a stranger's voice.

Your nose detects tiny **molecules** in the air and can pick up the tiniest whiff of a burger on a grill, or dog poop on your shoe. The taste buds on your tongue can also detect molecules and tell you how delicious a mango or a strawberry might be. Your sense of touch comes from pressure on nerve endings in your skin, so when you put your arm around your best friend, you feel the sense of closeness that only touch can bring.

This illustration represents the fact that our eyes are our most important sense and our lips, hands, tongue, and feet are the most sensitive to touch.

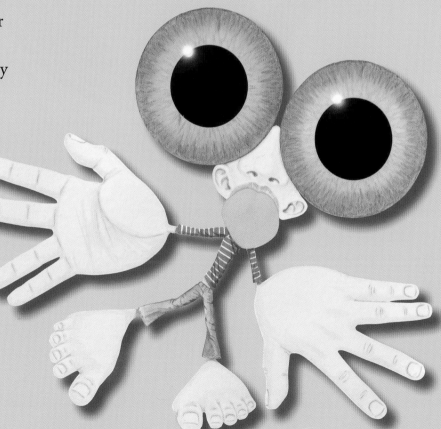

WHEN THINGS GO WRONG

Losing a Sense

Many people do not have all five senses. They may be born without one of them—usually sight or hearing. Sometimes people lose a sense during their lives as a result of an illness or because the sense has been damaged. Ear drums can be damaged by very loud noise and eyes are damaged if they receive too much **ultraviolet radiation** from the sun. People who have lost a sense may find that they can concentrate harder on their other senses. For example, people who lose their sight may learn to listen more carefully.

A Pair of Eyes

Your amazing sense of sight, or vision, allows you to do many things. You can catch a ball flying through the air, see a plane in the sky many miles away, read the words in a book, and tell the difference between millions of colors.

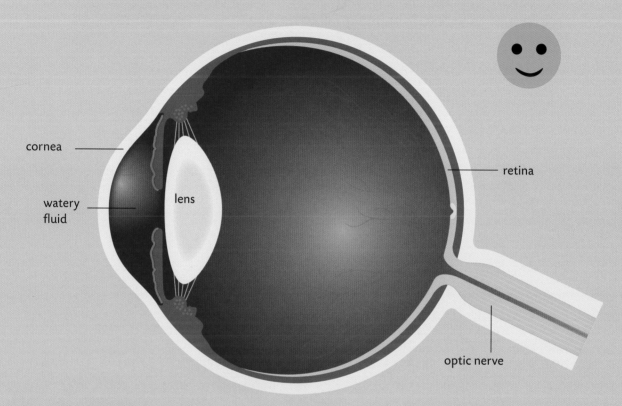

cornea

watery fluid

lens

retina

optic nerve

A Kind of Camera

Each of your eyes is like a small ball about 1 inch (2.5 cm) across that sits inside the front of your skull. It has six muscles that allow the eye to swivel from side to side and move up and down. Some people can look at their nose and go cross-eyed!

At the front of your eye, the eyeball has three transparent layers: a thin, curved cornea, a **lens**, and a little watery fluid

The retina that lines the inside of the eyeball contains nerve cells that are sensitive to light rays. A nerve called the optic nerve takes messages from these cells to the brain.

sandwiched in between. Together, these layers focus light rays onto the center of a layer called a **retina** inside the back of the eye. Light rays reflected from an object form an upside-down image on the retina, as if the eye were a kind of camera.

Everyone should visit an optometrist for an eye test from time to time. **Optometrists** can prescribe glasses or contact lenses for people whose eye lenses don't change shape enough—this can make them nearsighted or farsighted. People who are nearsighted need help to see distant objects. They often wear glasses when they are driving. People who are farsighted need help to see objects close to them, and they wear glasses to read books or browse the Internet. Optometrists can also detect other health problems, such as high **blood pressure**, by looking at the retina at the back of the eye.

The Changing Lens

The lens in your eye is stretchy and elastic. Muscles make the lens change shape so that it can focus light rays from objects that are near and far away. When you try to focus on something several hundred feet away, such as a tree on a hillside or a building on the horizon, the lens becomes flat. When you focus your eyes on a nearby object, such as a page in a book, the lens bulges and becomes more spherical (rounder). This process of changing the shape of the lens is called **accommodation**.

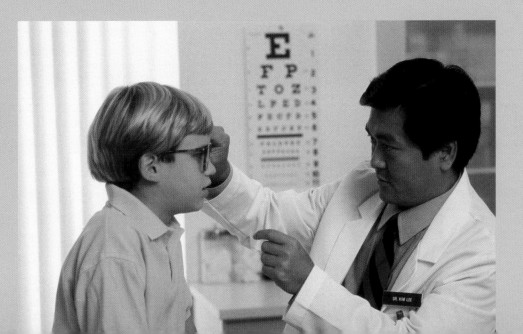

During an eye test, an optometrist can tell how well your eyes are working by checking the power of each lens to change shape.

Looking and Seeing

Your eyes are really part of your central nervous system. They detect the light rays reflected by objects or given off by lights such as a flashlight or traffic light, but it is your brain that does all the seeing.

Rods and Cones

The retina of the eye contains two kinds of nerve cells—**rods** and **cones**. They are called **receptors** and are very sensitive to light. Rods help you see things when the light around you is dim, for example, at night. The cones are grouped around the center of the retina. They work in bright light, when they allow you to see things in different colors.

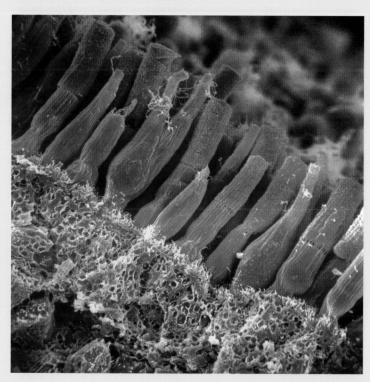

The retina contains many rods (green) and cones (blue).

Did You Know?

You have about 120 million rods and 6 million cones inside the retina of each eye.

Seeing With Your Brain

When light rays fall on the retina, they activate the rods and cones. These cells send electrical messages along the optic nerve from the back of the eyeball to your brain. This is where the image of the object you're looking at is really seen.

This brain scan shows what happens when the cells in a part of the brain called the visual cortex (red and white area at the top) are active.

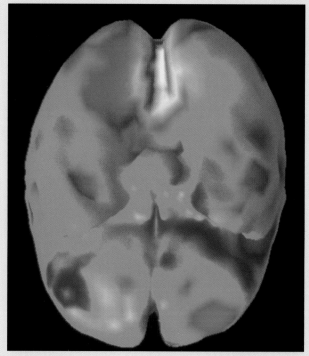

At the lower rear of your brain is an area called the **visual cortex**. Here, a number of cells put together an image of what you're looking at. Another part of the brain tells you what the object is. You can play tricks called optical illusions with the way your eyes and brain work together, and these can make you think you see things that aren't actually there.

Three Dimensions

Your two eyes set in the front of your head help you see in three dimensions. This gives you **stereoscopic vision**. If you look through just one eye, you see things in two dimensions, which means they look flat. Using stereoscopic vision, you can see the height, width, and depth of an object. This means you can see in three dimensions.

Each eye has something called a **field of view**. This is the area in front of you that the eye can see. Your left eye has one and your right eye has a different one. The two fields of view overlap in the center. Your brain "sees" objects in this central area in three dimensions, as though you were looking through a pair of binoculars.

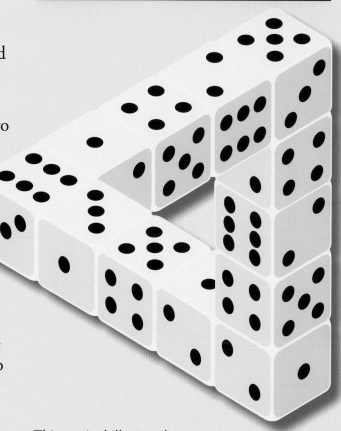

This optical illusion shows you how easy it is to fool your eyes into seeing what's not really there.

9

Inside Your Ears

You use your eyes more than any other sense, but you also rely on your ears to detect the sounds around you. Using your ears, you can listen to music, hear your phone ringing, and hear what your friends are saying.

Parts of the Ear

Your ear has three main parts: outer, middle, and inner. The ear you can see is the start of the outer ear. This leads to the eardrum. The other side of the eardrum is the middle ear where you will find the body's three tiniest bones, called the **ossicle bones**. These bones join the eardrum to a thin sheet or **membrane** called the oval window,

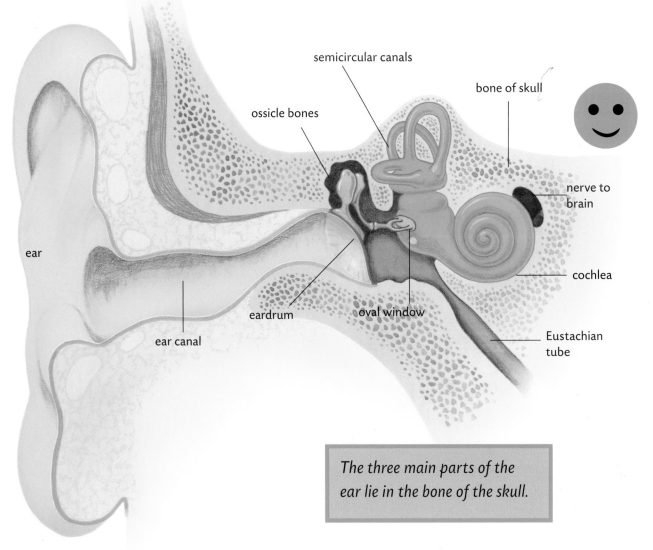

The three main parts of the ear lie in the bone of the skull.

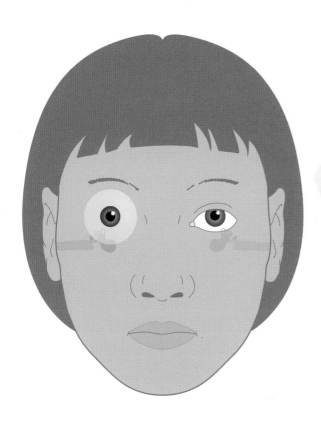

Did You Know?

Your eardrum is about the same size as your smallest fingernail—but much, much thinner.

Your middle and inner ears are beneath the bones of your face and run below your eyeballs.

where the **inner ear** begins. The middle and inner parts of your ear are deep inside your skull, which protects them. The middle ear is connected to your nose and your throat by a canal called the **Eustachian tube**.

The Inner Ear

Inside your inner ear is the cochlea, which looks like a tiny snail's shell. It is full of fluid as well as millions of tiny hairs and two very sensitive membranes. This is where sounds from the outside world are turned into nerve signals that go to the brain. Next to the cochlea are three loops called semicircular canals. These canals are very important in helping you to keep your balance (see pages 14–15).

What is Sound?

The sounds you hear are **vibrations** moving through the air as waves. When the waves are bunched up tightly, you hear a high sound. The amount of bunching up is called the **frequency**. The more the waves are bunched up, the higher the frequency and the higher the sound or the **pitch**. Waves that are spread out have a lower frequency and a lower pitch.

Hearing and Listening

Sounds make vibrations that travel through
the parts of your ear and are turned into nerve signals.
Your brain then interprets these signals and identifies
the sound—for example, the bark of a dog,
the crash of a wave, or the horn of a car.

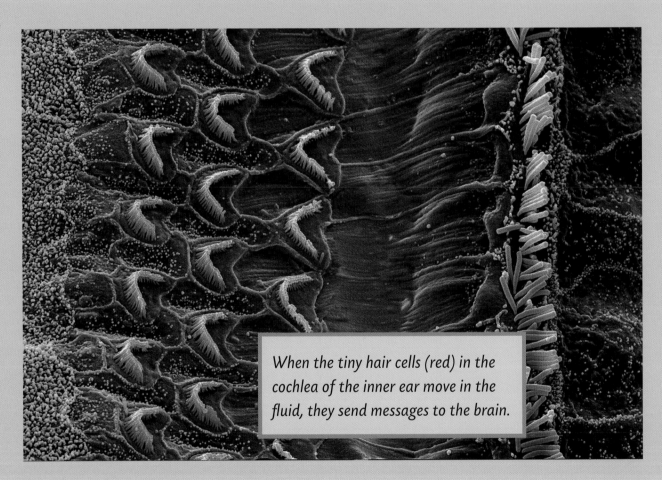

When the tiny hair cells (red) in the cochlea of the inner ear move in the fluid, they send messages to the brain.

Moving Waves

The waves from a sound enter your ear, where they move along the ear canal and set the eardrum vibrating. These sound vibrations are picked up by the three ossicle bones and passed on to the oval window of the inner ear.

As the oval window vibrates, it moves the fluid in the cochlea at the same frequency as the original sound that entered your outer ear. This vibrates the membranes and hair cells inside the cochlea (see above), which send messages as nerve signals to your brain. This part of the brain, called the auditory cortex, decodes the signals and hears the exact pitch and loudness of the sound.

Where's That Sound?

Your brain can tell which direction a sound is coming from and how far away it is. Having two ears helps. A sound directly in front of you or behind you reaches both ears at the same time. However, a sound on one side of you takes a fraction of a second longer to reach the ear on the other side of you.

WHEN THINGS GO WRONG

Damaged Eardrum

A hole or tear in your eardrum can hurt and cause hearing loss. An **infection** of the middle ear can make a hole if **pus** bursts through the eardrum. You can tear your eardrum if you poke something long and thin into your ear canal, if someone bangs you very hard on the ear, or if you hear a loud explosion. Sudden changes of air or water pressure can make a hole too. However, most damaged eardrums soon mend themselves.

The brain can automatically work out where the sound is coming from because of this tiny difference.

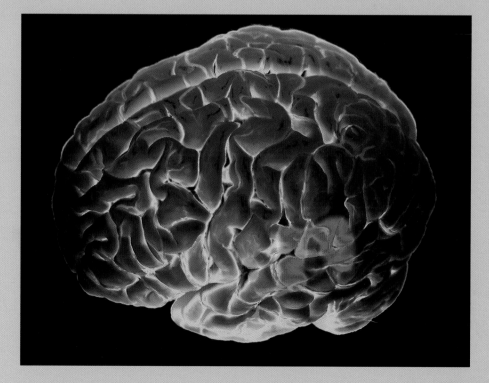

When a person listens to words, the cells in the auditory cortex part of the brain and an area just behind it (shown in red and green) become active.

Keeping Your Balance

Inside each of your inner ears is a structure that helps you to keep your balance. This is why you don't fall over when you move. The structure detects every movement your head makes and tells your brain how to change the position of your body.

A gymnast demonstrates perfect balance as he goes through his routine.

Hair Cells

The structure is called a **vestibule** and it is connected to the cochlea (see pages 12–13). Each vestibule has three curving canals and two spaces that are filled with a fluid that moves when your head moves. They also have tiny, delicate hair cells that bend when the fluid moves around them. When the hair cells bend, they send nerve signals to the brain.

The hair cells can sense when you are moving in one direction—for example, riding in a train or going up and down in an elevator. They can also sense the force of gravity, which helps you tell which way is up—for example, when you find yourself in total darkness.

Detecting Movements

The curving semicircular canals in both ears enable you to know the position of your head at any time. When you turn your head, the fluid and hair cells inside one canal sense the movement. If you spin around, you start to feel dizzy and lose your balance. This is because the fluid and hair cells in all three canals are trying to tell you where your head is. If you do lose your balance and fall over, the fluid and hair cells take a little while to settle down again.

A teenage girl uses an audiometer to test the sensitivity of her hearing.

HEALTH CHECK
Hearing Tests

People who are having difficulty with their hearing can have two kinds of tests. The first test looks at the eardrum and the bones of each middle ear. If these are working normally, the doctor will perform a second test, called **audiometry**, to find out if there is a problem in the inner ear. The person listens to a sound at a particular frequency—soft at first, then gradually growing louder. The person presses a button when he or she can hear the sound. This test is done at different frequencies and helps the doctor find out how much hearing a patient has lost and what the cause might be.

What's Up Your Nose?

You mainly use your nose to breathe. Most of your
nose is used to clean and warm the air before it enters
your lungs. Only a small part has a sense of smell.
This detects some of the molecules in the air.

Breathing In

When you breathe deeply through your
nose, the air goes up through your nostrils
into two spaces called **nasal cavities**. Inside
are lots of small hairs called **cilia** (say
"silly-a"), which push **mucus** toward the
back of your throat to be swallowed. This
mucus takes out bacteria and dust from
the air before the air goes into your lungs.

At the top of each nasal cavity just beneath
the bridge of your nose is a small area
called a cleft. A small patch of tissue
here is sensitive to many of the molecules

in the air. Inside the tissue are millions
and millions of tiny sensory hair cells
connected to cells called receptors.

*There are more than 20 million
tiny hair cells in the uppermost
cleft of your nose, lining its
surface. They are connected to
your olfactory bulb just above.
The hair cells detect scent
molecules in the air.*

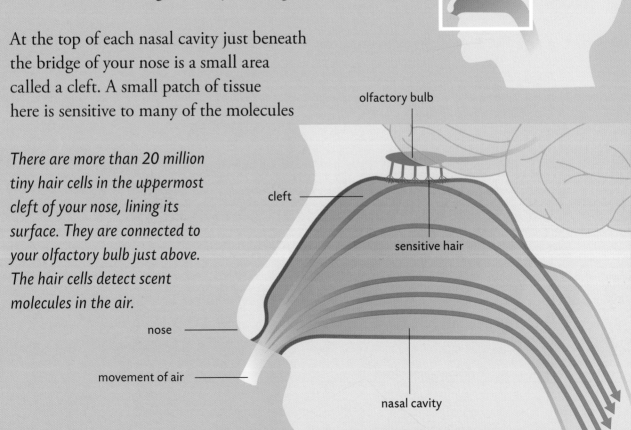

olfactory bulb

cleft

sensitive hair

nose

movement of air

nasal cavity

Detecting Smells

The air contains lots of different molecules. Some of these are picked up by the sensory hair cells that make the receptor cells produce nerve signals. These go to a part of your brain called the **olfactory bulb**. One bulb sits above each nasal cavity and sorts out all the nerve signals about smells before they are sent on to the smell center in your brain.

SNIFFING

When you breathe in through your nose, very little air reaches the cleft at the top of each nostril. But when you sniff, you speed up the air so more enters the cleft and comes into contact with the sensitive hair cells. This gives you a better chance of smelling what's in the air.

A woman moves her nose close to a newly opened rose to sniff its fragrance.

Air travels slowly through your nose during a normal breath and spreads through the nasal cavity (opposite). When you sniff to smell something (right), the air travels faster and more reaches the sensitive hairs at the top.

olfactory bulb

cleft

sensitive hair

nose

movement of air

nasal cavity

Why Smell Is Important

Think of all the smells that might float in the air around you, such as grilled bacon, freshly cut grass, a honeysuckle flower, peeled oranges, unwashed feet, cooked fish, boiled cabbage, and sour milk. The huge variety of smells you can detect show you just how important your nose is.

These fields of flowers are used to make lavender scent.

Different Kinds of Smells

The tiny sensory hairs connected to the olfactory bulb at the top of your nose can detect many different smells. So your sense of smell is more sensitive than your sense of taste (see pages 20–23). Some smells, such as lavender, are stronger than others. This is because they have the lightest molecules. Heavy molecules, such as candlewax, don't smell nearly as strong.

You use your sense of smell in various ways. Bad smells tell you that something is rotten—for example, milk that has gone sour or butter that is expired. The bad smell stops you from putting the food in

SMELLING SALTS

Smelling salts were very popular in the nineteenth century when British policemen carried them to revive anyone who fainted. When people lose consciousness, they can be revived by opening a small bottle of smelling salts under their nose. The salts release a chemical called ammonia, which irritates the lining of the nasal cavity and makes the lungs inhale hard.

your mouth and becoming ill from eating it. Pleasant smells help you appreciate your food. The aroma of good food wakes up your appetite and makes you realize how hungry you are. Warning smells, such as smoke or gas, tell you to beware of danger. Other smells are designed to attract attention, such as perfume or aftershave.

WHEN THINGS GO WRONG

Loss of Smell

Your sense of smell works best when you are young, and it becomes less sensitive as you grow older. Some people are born without a sense of smell. When you have a cold, or have an allergic reaction to something such as pollen, the entrance to the nasal cleft is blocked by mucus and you may lose your sense of smell for a day or two.

The bad smells from rotting food can be very strong. They are usually caused by bacteria breaking down the food.

On Your Tongue

Your sense of taste is similar to your sense of smell, except it comes from your tongue instead of your nose. The two senses often work together because they both detect chemicals in food and drinks. Between them, they send your brain messages that tell it which food and drinks you really like and which you can't stand.

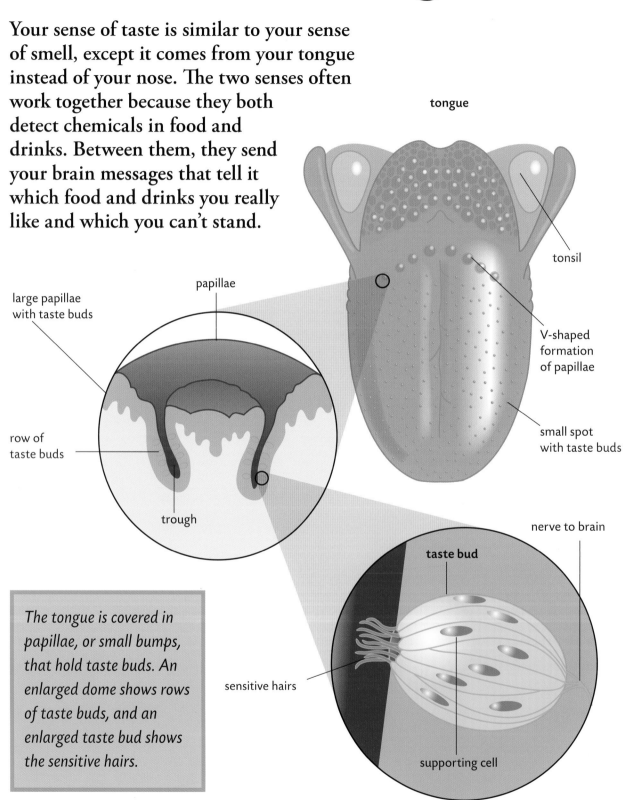

tongue

tonsil

V-shaped formation of papillae

small spot with taste buds

large papillae with taste buds

papillae

row of taste buds

trough

nerve to brain

taste bud

sensitive hairs

supporting cell

The tongue is covered in papillae, or small bumps, that hold taste buds. An enlarged dome shows rows of taste buds, and an enlarged taste bud shows the sensitive hairs.

Licking ice cream with your tongue is the best way to enjoy the flavor.

Papillae

Your tongue is an amazing **organ** made up of muscles that let you chew, swallow, suck, and talk. Stick out your tongue in

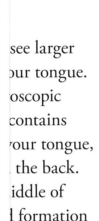

ee some
ese are used
are not

see larger
our tongue.
oscopic
contains
our tongue,
the back.
iddle of
l formation
pes. Each

f cells
layers
ve
eft).
liva
ls and
gnals to
what the

HOW MANY TASTE BUDS?

You have around 10,000 taste buds on your tongue. When you were a baby, you probably had some taste buds in your cheeks and on the roof of your mouth, too. Girls tend to have more taste buds than boys.

Did You Know?

A cat's tongue has bigger bumps than a human tongue. When cats lick and clean their fur, you can hear a rasping sound.

Tasting Food and Drinks

We can all detect four or even five different types of taste sensation. As you grow older, the way you taste food and drinks can change. This means that you may begin to like some food or drinks that you have never liked.

Four Types

When we chew a mouthful of food or sip a drink, we use at least four types of taste to help us identify it. These are sweet, sour, salty, and bitter. There may even be a fifth "savory" taste (see page 23). Every taste, whether it's chocolate, hamburger, cabbage, lemonade, ice cream, fish, or coffee, is more or less a combination of the four basic taste sensations.

Sugar, honey, and **saccharin** are sweet sensations. Vinegar, orange juice, and lemon juice give us sour sensations. We all recognize salty sensations. Coffee, unsweetened chocolate, olives, dandelion leaves, and tonic water create bitter tastes.

It was once thought that different areas of the tongue were sensitive to the four types of taste. We now know that all areas can detect the types of taste, although some areas seem to be more sensitive than others to particular sensations.

People have been adding herbs, spices, and seasonings to food for a very long time. The extra flavors added during cooking vary from region to region around the world and they help to stimulate our taste buds in many delicious ways.

Freshly chopped parsley can add flavor to many dishes.

Not Just Taste

Taste buds are not the only parts of your mouth that "tell" you about food and drinks. The upper and lower surfaces of the tongue, the inside linings of the cheeks, the mouth's roof and floor, and even the gums are all covered with touch-sensitive nerve endings similar to those in the skin. They detect whether food is hot or cold, hard or soft, smooth or lumpy, and many other sensations that add to taste.

Loss of Taste

Imagine what it would be like if you couldn't taste anything at all, especially if you lost your sense of smell as well. You might lose interest in food and drinks altogether. Problems with the sense of taste can be caused by taking some medicines or by a lack of vitamins. People who

Huge piles of spices for sale at a grocer's shop in India.

A FIFTH TASTE?

Some experts think that there is a fifth taste sensation. It is called umami, which means something like yummy, and it is linked with the savory flavors in foods. Examples of foods that cause you to taste the umami sensation are beef, lamb, soy sauce, and parmesan cheese.

smoke, or who are exposed to certain chemicals—or even radiation—can lose their sense of taste.

Sensing with Your Skin

Your skin covers the whole of the outside of your body and it is very sensitive to pain, vibrations, touch, and changes in the temperature around you. This sensitivity comes from millions of tiny nerve cells.

Inside Your Skin

Your skin has three main layers. On the outside is the epidermis and on the inside is a layer of fat. In between is the dermis, which contains blood vessels, hairs, and sweat glands. It also has glands that produce a waxy, oily substance called sebum. This waterproofs your skin.

In addition, there are millions of tiny nerve cells that send signals to your brain with information about the outside world.

Sensing Touch

Right at the top of the dermis, where it meets the epidermis, there are sensory nerve endings that are sensitive to light

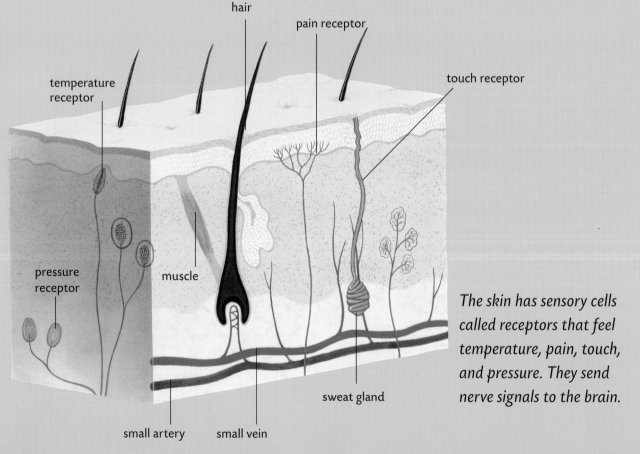

hair

pain receptor

touch receptor

temperature receptor

pressure receptor

muscle

sweat gland

small artery

small vein

The skin has sensory cells called receptors that feel temperature, pain, touch, and pressure. They send nerve signals to the brain.

touch, such as a kiss on the cheek or a pat on the back. Also, at the top of the dermis are nerve endings that detect vibrations like those created by drums in a rock band or by a truck driving by your home.

Nerve cells deeper in the dermis detect much stronger pressure on the skin. These are in the palms of your hands, on the soles of your feet, and on your lips, eyelids, and nipples. In the palm of your hand, these pressure receptor cells work when you grip something tightly, such as the handle in the car of a roller coaster.

HOW MANY NERVE CELLS?

Most of the sensory nerve cells in your skin let you feel pain (see pages 26–27). In one square inch of skin, there are around 1,200 of these cells (or around 200 per square cm), compared with just 15 that detect pressure, 6 that detect cold, and only 1 that detects warmth. Your fingertips probably have the most sensory nerve cells, and your lower back has the fewest.

Touch is an important way to show affection, as parents and their children often do.

Feeling Temperature and Pain

If you dip your finger into a cup of very cold water, you quickly realize that all the sensory nerve cells in your skin work together. It's hard to tell which sense works fastest: the touch of the water, or the cold that makes you want to take out your finger.

People wear coats, hats, and scarves in the winter to protect themselves from feeling the freezing cold.

Hot and Cold

Your skin has special nerve cells that detect the temperature of something placed near it or against it. Some cells detect warmth, while others detect cold. They allow you to feel the heat from a fire or the chill of a winter wind, the warmth of hot bath water or the cold of an ice cube pressed against your neck.

Pain in the Brain

Headaches and migraines affect many people around the world, causing them lots of pain. Research has shown that 50 percent of 7 to 15 year-olds suffer from headaches, and 10 percent of the same age group suffer from migraines.

The pain-detecting cells in this cook's hand sent a message to her brain when boiling water splashed on her.

These temperature-sensitive cells warn you about the dangers around you. Together with the cells that detect pain, they send nerve signals from your skin, telling the brain how close you are to something very hot or cold. This warning system helps to stop you from hurting yourself.

Ouch!

You feel pain from many sources, such as a toothache, a headache, a twisted ankle, a broken bone, a disease that damages your body's tissues—and even if someone pinches or slaps you.

When you feel pain, your body is telling you that something is wrong. Some pain doesn't last long and goes away if you take a painkiller such as aspirin or acetaminophen. Other pains can last a long time and can be very distressing.

The sensory nerve cells that register pain are all over your body, not just in your skin. Your tongue and eyes have lots of these pain cells, but your insides do not have very many.

When something triggers the cells, they send urgent messages to the spinal cord and the brain saying, "Ouch! That hurts!" until the brain does something about it.

Do You Have a Sixth Sense?

Some people believe that we have an extra sense that gives us information about events in the world in addition to our five other senses. It is difficult to prove scientifically that we have a sixth sense, but some especially sensitive people may have it.

Identical twins seem to have a sixth sense because one often knows what the other is thinking.

Extra Sense

Have you ever had a strong feeling that you know what someone is thinking, even though they haven't told you? Or have you ever sensed that something is about to happen before it does happen? If you have, you might have experienced a moment of **extrasensory perception**, or ESP.

One ESP power is called **telepathy**. This involves communicating with someone else without actually speaking to them. It's almost as though one person's brain

is talking to another person's brain—
a bit like a radio transmitter sending
information via waves to a radio receiver.

Seeing into the Future

Another ESP power is called clairvoyancy.
This is a process through which someone
can see into the future or dream about
an event that is about to happen. There
are many stories of people who avoid a
disaster, such as a plane crash, because they
have been warned about it in a dream.

Gut Feeling

Intuition is another part of the sixth sense.
Some people call this having a hunch or a
gut feeling. It means you feel or know that
something is true or right, even when you
don't have a good reason for it. Those who

SEEN IT BEFORE

People sometimes say, "I've seen
this happen already" when they see
an event taking place. This doesn't
mean they have experienced
extrasensory perception. This
sensation is called déjà vu (day-ja-
voo), which is French for "already
seen." What it means is that the
brain can see something and then
convince itself that it had seen it
before, all in the blink of an eye.

have good powers of intuition do not seem
to rely on their ordinary senses as much as
other people.

Fortune tellers claim they can
tell your future, but this is
very unlikely to be true.

Glossary

accommodation   The way the lens of the eye changes shape when it focuses rays of light inside the eye.

audiometry   A test that measures how well the ears hear various sounds.

blood pressure   The pressure of the blood against the walls of the arteries.

cilia   Tiny hairs in the lining of the nasal cavity and other body parts.

cones   Special cells, or receptors, in the retina that detect colored light.

Eustachian tube   A canal linking the middle ear with the throat. The Eustachian tube helps to stop pressure from building up in the middle ear.

extrasensory perception (ESP)   The ability to sense something in the world around you without using any of your five senses.

field of view   The area in front of you that one of your eyes can see.

frequency   The number of times a sound wave vibrates in a second.

infection   A disease caused by an invading organism.

inner ear   Part of the ear where sounds are turned into nerve impulses and where the body's position and balance are detected.

lens   The transparent part of the eye that focuses light rays on the retina.

membrane   A very thin layer inside or around a cell, or a protective covering for a row of cells or larger body part.

molecules   The smallest form of a chemical substance, such as oxygen.

mucus   A liquid made by the body to stop membranes from drying out.

nasal cavity   The space inside a nostril in the nose.

olfactory bulb   The organ of smell at the top of the nasal cavity.

optometrist   A doctor who tests eyes and makes glasses and contact lenses.

organ   A major part of the body that has one or more special tasks. The eyes, ears, heart, and lungs are all organs.

ossicle bones   The three tiny bones found in the middle ear.

papillae   The small bumps on the tongue that contain taste buds.

pitch   The frequency of a sound when it is heard by the ears. The pitch of a sound describes how high or low the frequency is.

pus   The thick yellow liquid that forms in an infected wound.

radiation   Rays of energy produced by something, such as the sun, a light bulb, or a radio transmitter.

receptors   Sensory cells that detect something in the world around them.

retina   A layer of cells that lines the inside of the eye and is sensitive to light. The retina contains special cells called rods and cones.

rods   Special cells, or receptors, in the retina of an eye that allow you to see light, but not colors. Rods help you to see in dim light.

saccharin   A manmade chemical for sweetening food and drinks.

stereoscopic vision   Seeing in three dimensions using both eyes.

stimulate   If you want to make something more active, you stimulate it.

telepathy   A type of extrasensory perception in which two or more people communicate directly without using the five senses.

ultraviolet   A type of high-energy radiation produced by the sun.

vestibule   Part of the organ of balance found in the inner ear.

vibrations   Regular, repeated movements of a substance such as air.

visual cortex   The place at the back of the brain where nerve signals from the retina in each eye are turned into images.

Books

Beck, Esther. *Cool Sensory Suspense: Fun Science Projects About the Senses* (Cool Science). ABDO Publishing Company, 2008.

Chancellor, Deborah. *I Wonder Why Lemons Taste Sour and Other Questions About the Senses*. Kingfisher, 2007.

Kalman, Bobbie. *What Senses Do Animals Have?* (Big Science Ideas). Crabtree Publishing Company, 2009.

Snedden, Robert. *Understanding the Brain and the Nervous System* (Understanding the Human Body). Rosen Central, 2010.

Web Sites

www.kidshealth.org/kid/stay_healthy/body/ear_care.html
Information on taking care of your ears and what happens when ears become infected.

www.exploringnature.org/
Find out more about the eyes, ears, and other senses.

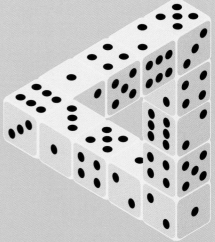

Index